THE EXCLUSIVE LAYGUIDE

WHEN DATING AND HAVING SEX WITH INCREDIBLY HOT WOMEN IS NO LONGER MIRAGE EVEN IF YOU DON'T LOOK LIKE A MODEL OR DON'T MAKE A FORTUNE

MICHAEL ANTONIO

Outskirts Press, Inc.
Denver, Colorado

The Exclusive Layguide
When Dating and Having Sex with Incredibly Hot Women is No Longer Mirage Even If You Don't Look Like the Models or Don't Make a Fortune

Outskirts Press, Inc.
http://www.outskirtspress.com

ISBN: 978-1-4327-1240-2

Outskirts Press and the "OP" logo are trademarks belonging to Outskirts Press, Inc.

PRINTED IN THE UNITED STATES OF AMERICA

TABLE OF CONTENTS

THE VARIOUS TYPES OF WOMEN

There are different types of women. Each of them is different from the rest, interesting and fascinating. Probably everyone has had the chance to fall in love with quite different types of women. Let us discuss the various types of women. Then, you can decide which one is suitable for you.

Starting with Ms Superior

This type of women advocates gender equality. They do not like men who love to dominate women. They are ambitious and always fight for their goals. They love to share equally everything with their partner. It is hard to understand what such a woman wants because she seldom lets her feelings out. She has strong character and displays independence. Often, such women reach pretty high hierarchical levels, sometimes they may be rather arrogant and it is dangerous

1

to joke with them because they take everything quite seriously. They like balanced men who know what they want.

Continuing with Ms Satisfied

This type of woman is always smiling, positive, jovial and full of energy. It is great to be around such a woman. When you are in bad mood, she will be the person to cheer you up. She knows how to converse with you on all topics and she is very amusing. When you come back home, she will meet you with a smile and she will make you a relaxing massage. She is always ready to support you and to stand by your side whatever is on the way. She is full of surprises and you will never be bored with a woman of this type. Her only flaw is that she is very obsessive. But, if you find such a woman, you'd better not leave her for she is a real treasure.

Following with Ms Passion

She is the type of woman every man dreams of. She always takes care of herself and she looks brilliant. She may be a great surprise in bed. She loves sex and she does not conceal it. She is experimenting and she has no holdbacks. When you come upon such a woman, you will find it hard to leave her, but it will be difficult to keep her, anyway. This type of woman is not constant. They love sex, but they also love diversity. They are *bon-vivant* and live for the moment.

They have no serious intentions, so it would be better if you do not invest any feelings in such a woman, but only amuse as long as you can.

now comes the turn of Ms Ideal

This type of woman is very self-confident, she looks well and she is communicative. She likes to visit cultural events, she can communicate with all types of men and she is very caring. This type of woman likes serious relations. When they find the proper man, they do everything to keep him, because they are ready to spend the rest of their life with him. She is pretty, intelligent, amusing and in any case might be the ideal wife for you.

Following with Ms Over-Confident

These women are often daughters of rich fathers. They always look perfect and never remain unnoticed. They may always be found in big companies and make friends with people from their social circle. If you like this type of woman and you wish to conquer her, the best approach is to ignore her. She is accustomed to be continuously courted by men; she is overwhelmed with thousands of compliments which do not impress her at all. However, if anyone appears who seems indifferent to her, she will be irritated and she will be the first to make the step. She loves to play mollycoddle and she is the perfect friend, if you wish to tell your friends a few home truths or to boost your self-confidence.

Ms Best Friend

Your characters are very similar. You love doing the same things. You like the same music, films etc. You feel free in her company. You don't bother what you say or what you look like, because she never makes you any remarks and never judges you about anything. She is always on your side. She is ready to help you when you are in need. She loves to have fun with you and she always laughs at your jokes. You will feel gorgeous with this type of woman because you will have both a good friend and a smart girl-friend.

Ms Independence

This type of woman follows her own life routine and she is rather independent. She got accustomed long ago to manage with everything by herself. She never relies on men and she does not need them because she copes perfectly on her own. She is the perfect choice for men who are very busy at their work and do not have enough time to spend on a relation. Such type of woman will never ask anything of you. Whatever happens with your relations, she will accept it with absolute calmness.

and last, Ms Direct

She is of the type of women who use to tell everything in your face. She has no holdbacks and she is not ashamed of anything. She is a tough girl and she may sometimes be rude. You will be never entangled in her thoughts, because she will tell you directly everything. She loves noisy companies and heavy beer-drinking. She is not very feminine, but she is of that type of women, with whom you will feel most free, without any holdbacks.

It is up to you to decide which type of woman you will choose. The most important thing is that she makes you happy.

EVERYTHING STARTS BY FLIRT

How can women be attracted? Men are known to like by their eyes, however, women like by their heads.

If a woman is aware that somebody is out for her only to take her to bed, her place will definitely be not there. Though it is clear that, anyway, the target remains there, there are much gentler ways to get to bed that the direct announcement. I doubt when the direct "Shall we go to bed?" would do, but for the case where the subject in question is some crocodile who has never heard a gentle word in her life or she belongs to the type of women who are interested only in your money.

Therefore, one should flirt. Flirt is more than art. Flirt is a manner of behaviour, a manner of communication, a manner of attitude and what is more than friendly attitude towards the person in front of you. However, flirt is not:

"You are very sexy. Shall we go to bed?"

Flirt is a way to attract a person you like, to try, at least a little, to come to know him/her, as well as to give him/her a chance to know you. Slight wink and wide smile, they both flirt.

The purpose of the flirt is not necessarily to take someone to bed. A casual flirt may win you many more friends. It may help you succeed where you would not have succeeded otherwise. And word does not go about sex alone, because flirt brings both participants closer at a level where no conversations would have drawn them.

In the casual flirt version you show that you are not indifferent to the person in front of you, in terms of his **looks** and character. When flirting, you are not obliged to reach to the end. When flirting, you at least increase the level of the hormones of happiness and satisfaction, you prove to yourselves that you are smart, and you simply continue ahead.

The best friendship between a man and a woman always starts by a flirt, because when you like somebody, this is the best way to show it to him. It is a matter of choice and circumstances how the flirt will proceed.

However, when flirt's rate slows down, the two start to build other relationships, usually friendly and open ones.

Open relationships, however, does not mean sharing bed. And when flirt deepens and continues, then, the ultimate goal will be much more passionate and intimate.

Flirt boldly. And don't forget that flirt is an art to communicate and a weapon to gain easier victories.

What Do Women Like About Men?

Have you asked yourselves what things about men attract women? Smile? Muscles? Clothes? Self-confidence? Or all of these?

When a man has a crash on some woman, he does everything to make her like him. He often asks himself what she would like in him. He always wants to play himself best, to be smart, amusing, sexy etc.

Recently, women's requirements for men increased greatly, compared to the past. Now women want men to be strong, caring, well-bred, self-confident, successful, and many more.

You may have a tight bottom, but you are not deep-chested and you wonder whether she will like you because you don't have the complete list with the requirements for you. The truth is that every woman likes different type of men. Of course, the features mentioned above appeal to all women, but this doesn't mean that if you do not possess them all, she will not like you. It all depends on what she is after at the moment. Some day you may look super sexy to her, and on the next day she may not think that at all. If she is merely looking for a man to have an exciting night with, she will most probably be after a well-looking man. She will not give a damn whether he is self-confident, successful etc. She will care only about his tight bottom or deep chest. What I mean is that, if a woman is looking only for flirt, she may choose some genuine, not very clever macho, but if she looks for something more serious, she will rather prefer someone not looking like a model, but with whom she can talk on any topic.

When we, men, discuss the ideal woman, we always say that she must have big breasts and she must be blonde. But do we always date such women? Do we really like such women? This is simply an emblem, which though false, we always comment with our friends. It is the same with women. If you ask them what men they like, they will most probably enumerate such features that only popular Hollywood stars boast of. But, actually, they date quite different types of men.

Women want men to be both manly and sensitive, to manifest strength and at the same time to be able to show up their emotions. Actually, if a woman feels a man close by talking with him, she will be much more likely to step to physical intimacy. With women, things originate more often in the brain and not in other places, as it is with men.

As to manliness, the different women perceive it in a different way. Some may want the man to be more sexually aggressive; others may believe that the manly man should necessarily have muscular body; and third may fancy a gentleman with polished manners. Therefore, it would be best for you to be a little of all that. Thus, you will look manly in the eyes of all women.

As all women, every man likes looking sexy. This is not that difficult, if you maintain a seemly appearance. This means to have a good look in the glass before going out. Your clothes should not be crumpled, the colours should match, your hair should be styled, in other words, you should make so as to feel perfect in your skin. Look brilliant on the outside to feel brilliant on the inside. Besides, you will look more attractive, if you smile.

It is good to be yourself, to not overplay, because women recognize easily unnatural behaviour and this does not make them good impression. But if you behave yourself, this will definitely be sexy.

How Can You Attain the Thing Women Find Irresistible Confidence

As you already came to know, women find it most attractive when a man is confident. But becoming confident is not that easy. You can't buy or imitate it. So, how can a man acquire this magic quality which attracts women like a magnet?

Now, you will learn the things which will immediately launch up your confidence in communicating with women and you will become the charming man all women are dreaming of.

What a woman really wants in a man is confidence,

i.e. the trump-card is self-confidence.

Confidence… does not mean arrogance, superiority, meaningless showing off, or a swaggering macho. Women like men with genuine confidence.

Confidence, as you know, is a manner of thinking. In particular, man's confidence is often manifested as the „I can do it" attitude. This does not mean denying emotions. This does not imply lack of doubt, fear or vulnerability. It does not require any illusion of self-sufficiency.

Confidence simply says: „I can do it… somehow… at least, I can do the best I can". The confident attitude should not be permanent, it simply should be present on the overall with the most life challenges.

Over the hundreds of ears of human development, it was never so difficult for men to develop and manifest confidence as it is now, because in the past, confidence was needed to survive. Then, men simply had no great choice. Until recently, strive for physical survival was the major motive in establishing a couple and the roles of both genders were much more apparent. Here, we don't mean survival under extreme circumstances, however.

In the small societies we lived before, everyone could see the skilled hunter, stock-breeder, the brave defender, craftsman, leader, the wise teacher, the man who does not surrender to hardships. This is the visible manifestation of the principle „I can do it". Not outspoken, but clear and visible to everyone.

Unfortunately, however, nowadays the signs of genuine man's confidence are confused and gender roles are in a chaotic mish-mash. External manifestations of natural confidence have mixed up with the simple substitutes of consumer status symbols. But... women instinctively search for hidden marks of men's confidence level... and test how far it goes... but not in the traditional old-fashioned way.

And now, the good news! Since confidence is the primary attitude in meeting challenges of kinds, and there are challenges nowadays, the basic attitude of confidence may be cultivated and demonstrated. But it cannot be replaced by money, outer appearance or material belongings.

The willingness to take „battles" continues to be the major key to women's respect. Nowadays, a man can express his dynamics in many traditional ways, such as competence in his work, education, sports, hobbies, coping with children or making small repair works at home. Here, we may include anything that requires some skill, attaining a new one or overcoming the ego's uncertainty.

One can also proceed in the old-fashioned way by exposing himself to risks, jumping with parachute, practicing fighting sports, running snowboard, lifting weights, climbing rocks, overcoming political conflicts, starting a new business with more enthusiasm than money... However, these are merely means. It is not the specific activity that is important here, the important thing is to display the confidence of knowing (or what he thinks he knows) what to do.

Or... he may skip the really dangerous experience and undertake what actually is the Great Risk, emotional challenges. The man may choose to gain confidence on women themselves, which sometimes is more risky than rock climbing.

Despite women like the idea of a man being able to manage with many things, what really matters to her is his ability to manage with her. A genuine, mature woman will never bind herself to a man who is afraid of her sexuality, intellect or emotions.

This does not mean achieving a combination of confidence and compassion for women at all levels. And since this is one of the most risky adventures, the award is naturally among the greatest ones: the love of an affectionate woman who makes daily life a comfortable place. Confidence towards women - beautiful, plain, clever, pleasant, old, young or unpleasant, is a general attitude; this is a social skill which may and should be attained, if you wish to achieve a full-value relationship in your life and stop asking yourself the question „What actually women want?"

A lot of men cannot appreciate the qualities they possess. They do not spare themselves and this obstructs their confidence. If this is your case, the best thing to do is to write on a piece of a paper the qualities you pride in. You have a handsome body? Marvellous sense of humour? Intellect? You have so many qualities women would appreciate. Whenever you feel vulnerable or self-unconfident, you may produce this quality list and reread it and not before long you will see your confidence and your spirits rising up. Note down the things a woman would like in you repeat to yourself what a good choice you are, actually.

Have you happened to meet an incredibly beautiful woman and not be able to keep your head? We, men, are used to pay great attention to women's looks and often forget about their other qualities. This incredibly beautiful woman may be a mutton-head, have an awful sense of humour or be a total failure in bed? The next time you meet such a woman you'd better remember that chance is great she is not that ideal and behave to her just the same way as to any other woman. Thus, you will become the composed and confident man she herself would like.

You must have noticed that the most confident men are often leaders. If you wish to become confident, you must behave as a leader, too. When you go on a date, never ask her where she wishes to go and what she wishes to do. Don't leave the decision on her. You must be the one who always tells where and how; show her that you have assumed control of things. Thus you will be the resolute and energetic person women like.

Repeating successful steps may also boost your confidence. For instance, if you have taken your former date to some restaurant that she liked very much, you can invite the new target of your cravings to the same restaurant. Thus, you will be confident that the place has been tried already, moreover, successfully. If you have talked with some girl and the topics have been predisposing for both of you, you'd better remember this conversation and apply it to the next woman. So, whenever you find something that impresses a woman, be sure to remember it during your next meetings.

Confidence gets also enhanced when you overcome your fears. One of men's fears is to address an unknown woman, because they may be rejected and no one likes to be rejected. Take this as a challenge and attack your fears. If another fear of yours is to call her on the phone, then you should immediately pick up the receiver and call her. If you do regularly what makes you anxious, you will not only overcome your anxiety but you will be proud to overcome your fears. Each subsequent victory will add up to your confidence and women will notice it for sure.

Help people in need. If somebody has problems with his car, stop and help him. Surely, he will be very grateful for your help and this will definitely boost your confidence. Such acts will create in you the feeling that you are a good and reliable man, and this, on its part, will affect your confidence with women.

Learn to dance well. As you know, most people believe that if a person dances well on the dancing-floor, this means that he/she will quite probably dance as well in bed. When you dance well, all women will fix their eyes on you and this will immediately charge your confidence. Women adore men with regular movements, who can enjoy dancing, for this makes them self-confident.

It often happens that when a man talks with a woman he does not know whether she likes the conversation or it makes her feel bored. Such thought can only ruin your confidence and the woman will feel this immediately and retreat. Your conversation might have been very interesting to her, but when you lose confidence, this makes her lose interest. Next time when you talk with a woman, it would be good if you stop analyzing every word and expression of hers, but just relax and amuse yourself. Conversation is not exam that you must pass for sure. The more careless and composed you feel, the more confident you will actually become and the more women's attention you will attract.

Another thing that will make you extremely confident is to date and communicate with many women. When you talk with one woman in the morning, with another at noon, you will see yourself how much easier your conversation with the third one will be. You will become much more composed in women's presence and you will talk with every new one with no anxiety whatsoever. Moreover, if things do not go well with one woman, you will readily have a spare version and will never be left on the wrong side of the door. Thus, you will increase your options. This will help you get relaxed, amused, and irradiate the confidence women like so much.

One of the most efficient ways to boost your confidence is to improve your looks. It would be good to have good-quality, genuine-brand clothes and accessories in your wardrobe. Do not save money on clothes, because it is through them that you create the first impression with women. Your shoes must be always polished, your nails clean, your hair styled, and you should necessarily give out the smell of good perfume. If you feel smart on the outside, you are sure to emit positive and sexy signals which women will catch immediately. You will be surprised to see how the improvement of your looks will affect your confidence and your success with women.

When you look perfect in your skin, date with many women, you behave composedly with all of them and you don't get panicked by anything or by anybody, you are not anxious about what you will say or whether women find the conversation interesting or not, then, you surely will look confident and this will only draw women mad.

And, for the purpose of avoiding any doubt whatsoever regarding the sense of the foregoing, I will venture to summarize it like that:

Don't ask a woman what she wants, if you are not clear about what you want yourself.

What Does It Mean To Be a Real Man in the True Sense of This Word?

Is it enough to be confident, in order to be a real man? Some men feel like that when they smack women on their behind, whistle to them, cry like mad at football matches, boast how much they can drink without getting drunk, drive like mad, behave arrogant and other things like that. But whether these things make them real men?

The truth is that the real man has several major features which make him such. He must necessarily earn his money himself. He should never rely on a woman or a rich daddy to support him. If, anyhow, he starts a business with his father's money, he should multiply them several times, in order to be called a real man.

Women are very emotional and often cry. But the real man cannot afford to cry like them or whine. He never complains and never looks for someone else to solve his problems. He is the head of the family and he is always strong and respected.

The real man talks brief and clear. He does not go into unnecessary details. He never talks bad about the rest and tries to be positive to everyone. He always keeps his promises. People can always rely on him and they know that he will not mislead them.

The real man is concentrated and purposeful. He chases his dreams to the end. He has true friends on whom he can rely, but his family ranks first. He brings well his children and he is their model.

He can get well with all people, but if somebody offends his family, he is ready to play rude to defend them. He behaves as a gentleman with all women, but he would never do anything that might hurt his friend or wife.

Putting it briefly, to look like a real man in women's eyes, you should not be emotional, you should not weep, you should not talk bad about the people, you should not be weak, you should not rely on someone else to support you, you should not be lazy, irresponsible, you should not be a playboy with no goals.

The real man looks physically and psychically strong and caring and responsible, one who makes his way in life by himself, who trusts himself and the support of his family. He helps those in need and he always defends his friends. He is gentle to the ladies and he inspires strength and respect.

THE THINGS YOU SHOULD BE CAREFUL NOT TO OVERDO WITH

Men always want to make impression on women, but they often go too far projecting themselves and become funny on the eyes of the fine sex. There is nothing bad in the desire to look ideal to women, but there are certain limits you should obey.

As you already know, women are impressed by men who can dance well. There is nothing bad to know a couple of dances. But it will be too much if you start going to dance classes alone, if you are the first to appear on the dancing-floor, if you dance with your male friend, or if you are too energetic in your movements.

Naturally, before going out to head for a date, you'd better take care of yourself. But this does not mean that you should use women's cosmetics, pluck your eyebrows, and spend five hours before the looking-glass. You may also know some things about women's fashion, as well as what suits you, but to know when and where there is clothes' discount or to walk all day long about the shops, as women do, is inadmissible.

It is good if you can make various types of cocktails to serve on the chicks, who come to your place. You will not impress them, however, if you drink the same cocktails, such as Margarita, Bailey's etc, instead of choosing something hard like whisky, gin, vodka etc.

It is important to be attractive and to have a liking for fashion, but it is funny if you discuss before other people the other men's looks. Such as, for instance, to tell that some man is wearing shoes by a well-known designed and to tell that they would match you better.

As you already understood, the real man never cries. If it happens that you have fight with somebody and then you become upset and start crying, this will be definitely funny. Imagine going with your girlfriend to the cinema where you watch some sentimental film and then you shed some tears. It is not enough to say you will look stupid. Crying on some definite occasions like a wedding, a funeral, a concert etc. is also admissible. As a rule, it looks as if the real man is not allowed to cry at all.

The man is obliged to keep good hygiene. But this does not mean to super indulge in it, such as, for instance, when you shake hands with somebody, to try to wash your hands immediately afterwards or to make your guests always take down their shoes before entering your house.

There is nothing bad, as well, to have fun with your friends and to be all the time around them. But it will definitely be funny, if you head for the WC with your friends. You should always go there alone. The fact that women always go there in company does not mean that men should do the same. If you meet a girl you like it will be good to remain tête-à-tête with her. You don't need your friends' company.

You can also wear stylish accessories, such as a belt or a nice watch, but if you put on several rings and chainlets, then you will definitely become a laughing stock, unless your style is the rapper's one. Keep to this advice and then you will not look ridiculous before women.

Training
Techniques Which
Will Make You
Confident and
Composed

It is very important to learn to manage with confusing situations. Of course, this is not simple at all, but with practice you can achieve anything. One of the things that often stress us is meetings. We are always in suspense and feel like students at our first date. We feel unassured, because we don't know how we shall present ourselves. Whether she will like us, whether she will feel amused and other depressing doubts of this kind, of which we already spoke.

To avoid feeling confused in such case you'd better prepare in advance. Imagine that you are already at the meeting, choose a topic for conversation, and make a plan of everything that may be ahead. A brief plan that will make you feel more composed. Thus, you will not have to extemporize and will not fall into awkward situations.

You may exercise your confidence by going to a bar alone. Take a drink, be cool and focused. Don't look at your watch for some time and do not look around for some friend. Do not take out your mobile to get distracted and to pretend you are engaged in doing something. Just sit at the bar, consume your drink and try to concentrate, so that nothing can impress you. Try as well to overcome the curious staring at those around, paying no attention to them. When you start feeling more comfortable, you can increase the trial's hardship by going alone to the cinema or to the theatre, which will help you completely overcome the annoying anxiety.

When you get accustomed to go wherever alone, you will feel a hundred times more confident at the actual meeting. And during the meeting it will be good if you make some stand against the girl. It is not good to always agree with what she says. Thus, the meeting will turn from "fair to middling" to a really promising one.

The confident man is not afraid to contradict the woman he likes. This can only impress her because she will tell to herself that this man has confidence and though he likes her, he is not afraid to contradict her opinion.

Naturally, this does not mean that you should behave with her like that all the time. Show her that you like her by flirting with her. Thus, you both show her that you find her attractive, but you have the courage to oppose her as well. There is no other tactic so kindling as this one.

When you are on a date with a beautiful woman, you should be aware that she is hearing all the time all sorts of bombastic compliments. So, if she hears something like that from you, she will hardly be much impressed. Therefore, you should try to make your compliments different from the rest. Try to be a little unordinary. For instance, when she comes back from the WC, tell her how gracious her walk is. Or tell her that she has an incredible style and taste for fashion. This will encourage her, because most probably, she has spent an hour wondering what to dress to look well. Be inventive with your compliments. Thus, she will feel your individuality and she will not compare you with all her other suitors. Your interesting flatter will boost her self-confidence, which will predispose her to answer your feelings.

After the first date, a confusing situation is sure to arise when you tell her "Goodbye" with handshaking. This can be avoided, if you pave the way for something else during the whole evening.

While you are talking, touch her hand. Thus, you will see her reaction. If she has liked you, she will not withdraw. She will even feel very good. It is true that you are still quite a long way from the major thing, but you will see that even the touch of her hand may give you a great pleasure. As the saying goes, love starts through the hand, passes through the mouth and ends between the legs.

If at this stage she touches your knee or caresses your hand, this is a sure sign that things are going in the right direction.

In this case, you may freely end the date by a kiss. If you don't press her for anything more than a kiss, this will only make her want you all the more and you will collect positive score for the next date. And what is even better, you may show her that the initiative is still hers by asking her to call you.

The Fashion Style You Should Follow, If You Wish to Be Perfect in Everything

According to women, the first things they notice in a man are his watch and his shoes. Therefore, always wear a nice watch. You wish women to be impressed by you, don't you? The stylish watch matches well both sports and classic clothes. As for all other accessories, you needn't waste much money on them, but with respect to the watch you should not be thrifty.

After the nice watch come the well-polished shoes. Remember well that this is one of the main things women spot immediately. Shoes help a man to be distinguished among the crowd. They give out much more features about his character than the other parts of his clothes. First, never put on trainers. At some more casual places people might not be too critical about it, but you'd better put on stylish shoes which are suitable for a marriage party, for instance. There is no explanation for it, but women may choose a man only by the condition of his shoes. So, you see how important it is that they are clean and, if possible, a piece of a well-known designer. I hope it doesn't turn out that you are ready, dressed, with your perfume on, and only then you notice that the shoes you intend to put on are covered with such dust or mud that you can easily write not only your name, but draw something on them as well.

In this case, you will have to take to the not-so-clean work of placing your shoes in normal condition; but while doing this, your own condition will drop somewhere below the level of your not-so-clean soles. You may wear either black or brown shoes, but giving preference to brown ones will surely not leave you unnoticed and will immediately pull up your rating.

The socks you choose should match your shirt, trousers and shoes. They must be simple, single-coloured, or with thin stripes. I would advise you not to choose light colours, but to prefer neutral ones, such as black, brown, dark-blue, or grey. The socks should be long enough to exclude the possibility for your leg hair to appear above them. Put on warm socks, especially if you are going to date a girl. You wonder why? Because, if your legs get cold, your whole blood will run downwards to warm them and thus, it will omit the place that needs it most.

On daily occasions you may put on stylish designer's jeans or, if the event is an official one, trousers. Regarding the shirt, you have multiple options – more than with any other part of your clothes. If the weather is warm, you can put a short-sleeved shirt. A shirt with buttons and long sleeves is suitable for official occasions. Pullovers can do as well, but they should be one-coloured or in thin stripes.

Your tie should match the cloth of the lapel. If you wear a Papillion, it should be necessarily black. Don't wear too thin ties.

Your top garment must be chosen in accordance with the weather forecast. The jacket is worn on more informal occasions, and the coat – on more formal ones. The scarf is always worn under the coat.

As for your underwear, if there is the slightest possibility to remain in it, then let it be good. And the best attitude is to expect the unexpected. You can never know when some smart chick ready for sex will appear, and naturally, in such case you would wish to be comme-il-faut.

If you have pulled your shirt into your trousers, you should necessarily put on a belt. But if you have left it to fall freely and your waist cannot be seen, then you can do without a belt. Remember that your belt and your shoes should be of one and the same shade.

After the clothes, comes the turn of the good fragrance. Women adore men who emit the scent of some expensive perfume. Put enough of it, so that it can be smelt at no more than an arm's distance. Now you can take your credit cards, personal documents, keys, chewing gums, mobile, condoms and whatever else you deem necessary.

Most men have the habit to style their hair after they are ready. This is a bad practice since if you use gel for the purpose, a couple of drops might fall onto your perfectly clean shirt, which will loosen some "gentle words" on your side, then you will have to dress again and most probably, will be late.

If you wish to be absolutely in the fashion, you'd better wear only credit cards instead of a wallet with money. You may have noticed that the exquisite wealthy men wear only credit cards with them, and their cash is held on a clip.

If you follow these basic principles, you will feel really

well in your clothes and you will always look stylish and high-level. You will not be the crank, whom everybody regards with despise, but you will be a source of admiration, especially for women. As for the men, they'd sooner envy you.

THE THINGS YOU THINK WOMEN DO NOT NOTICE

You happen to mock women before your friends about the time they lose on beauty care procedures, but you should guess that they are doing it for you, men.

There are a lot of things which do not impress men very much, especially when it comes to hygiene. But when it comes to hygiene, women are particularly watchful and it is hardly possible that their eyes (or sooner, their nose) would miss such a thing as smelling stocks.

And really, imagine that after you have been to a restaurant and then – to a cinema, in the end, she has invited you to her place and when you take down your shoes, your socks emit a slight odour. In most cases, men believe this to be a small problem that can be neglected and think that the lady will not feel it, but actually, this is not so.

A great part of men don't pay attention to some parts of their body. This is not correct. Women are very particular and notice everything. If they don't like just a single thing in your looks, they are ready to stop dating you.

If you have eyebrows crossing like a bridge, then you surely must correct them. No woman expects of you to have eyebrows like hers, but they should not be overgrown, anyhow. It would be best to pluck them using a pincette and you will be surprised to see how the removal of just a couple of hairs will make you look much different.

The condition of your hands also prompts a woman what is your general hygiene. This does not mean that you should have your nails manicured every week.

Just buy a nail-rash and maintain your nails with it. No woman likes to be touched by jagged nails. But there is no woman who does not like to rub herself against gentle and soft skin. So, take care of your hands and nails, especially in winter. The nail-rash and the hand lotion will make your skin and nails brilliant and will be eager to touch you.

There are some things which may repel a woman 100% and these are fungi, uncut nails and odour. If you have one of these things, it means that your sexual life is lame for sure. If you believe that when hidden well in shoes and socks your feet are no problem, you are wrong.

You can't be hiding your feet in your shoes all the time, because at some moment you'll have to take them down. To avoid falling in some awfully shameful situation, buy a feet powder or ointment. And if this does not help, you may consult a doctor, but if you have no such problems, just try to take care of the other things which do not remain unnoticed by the fair sex.

Now comes the turn of hair. Recently, it became modern for men to get dehaired everywhere. A great part of the women like it, but there are still some who prefer more hairy men, because they find it more masculine.

Imagine a lady with hair under her nose, or putting it briefly, with moustache. Such a lady applies all possible efforts to get rid of it. Either by bleaching it or by applying a colo-mask, but she finds a way. Why don't you try, either? Anyhow, you should admit that hair sticking out of the ears and nose is not among the sexiest things you would like to be proud of.

If you don't want to remove your breast hair, then at least get rid of those in your armpit. Thus, when you sweat, you will not smell that much.

Teeth are exclusively important as well. One smile may win her heart. One smile may as well draw her away from you for ever, especially, if it reveals yellow or crooked teeth. It is inadmissible to have bad breath either, but using chewing gum will not save the situation. The solution is to visit frequently your dentist.

And last comes the back. Though you don't pay great attention to it, your back has the chances to become one of the sexiest parts of your body for her.

Anyhow, don't forget that this will not be true, if it is covered with hair, dead skin and acne. You can take care of the acne buying some anti-acne lotion and applying it on your back.

You can remove dead skin cells using an exfoliating cream. Hair is not among the greatest problems for it can be removed by a single visit to a beauty salon.

Why Women Have a Crash on Machos

Women choose their partner by his face oval. As you already know, they prefer strong, manly features. According to studies men with square jaw and bulging eyebrows are preferred for brief and stormy experiences. They are irresistible and attract all women around them.

This type of masculine men is more inclined to violence, insubordination and betrayal. However, women as a rule, not thinking much about it, are more willing to give themselves to the more masculine type of men, though anticipating that it will be for short.

And men with more feminine features, with rounder and pudgy faces and thick lips can be more trusted for a more long-lasting commitment, often resulting in marriage. They

40

are perceived as reliable potential fathers and spouses, industrious, loving and caring for the woman next to them.

The development of manly features depends on testosterone. Consequently, the manlier the outer appearance is, the greater the amount of testosterone. And when testosterone abounds, some man have a tendency for betrayal and violence in the relations with their partner. Therefore, despite they produce good-quality offspring, in a number of cases, extramarital, usually they are not among the best parents and faithful husbands. Probably, because due to their physical characteristics, they are spoiled by women and believe that they are allowed anything.

While the other type of men compensates for what nature has not endowed them with, with more intellect, tact, tenderness and devotion, so as to be able to keep the woman longer with them.

As a whole, the fair sex is almost unanimous nominating men's positive features, while enumerating a number of unpleasant ones, starting with their greater impulsiveness and quite emotional expression to the bad habit of smoking after sex.

The first thing women point out is that they love the man they are with, and this is the most important reason to close their eyes, when they are getting on their nerves. A woman is always ready to forgive a man who is charming and tender and who knows how to cheer up his beloved at times of strain. Women like men who make them feel secure and confident that whatever they do, they will succeed. A man who wins women always reckons with their wishes, even they be mere whims. He has a sense of humour and he is always the life and soul of the company. At home he is a strict but caring father admired by his children. He gets on well with his relatives and he loves pets.

On the other hand, women seldom put up with men who are ready to do everything for their friends, despite this would mean a row with their spouse. They are also annoyed by men who are workaholics and to whom office obligations rank first.

This type of men often expresses his intent to have fun until early in the morning, but in the evening he is too tired and prefers to go to bed. He behaves as a master in the kitchen and still manifests painful affection for his parents. Sometimes, he wouldn't listen to his partner's advice for which he is sorry later on.

For him, a stroll means to go by car to some place, drink a coffee there and then, come back home. He behaves like a child at times – he rides the high horse before his friends and tells things that never happened.

It depends on you how you will behave with a woman, but if

you want to keep her you definitely should not do the above mentioned unpleasant things. The more you practice to be attentive and positive with women, the greater success you'll have with them.

First Date – How to Impress Her So that a Second One Follows

The first date is the time when a woman understands whether she wants to be with this man or not. As you know, everything depends on the first impression.

Therefore, if you go out for the first time, you must present yourself in the most favourable light, however, not pretending to be something you are not. Thus, you will have greater chances to have a second date.

It is very important what place you have chosen for the date. She will surely pay attention to this, if she has not suggested it herself. But, as we talked already, the real man controls things and he does not let the lady to choose.

If you take her to some expensive place, using the money you have saved for cases of emergency, this will not be the best move on your part. By taking her to a place which is beyond your abilities merely to show her that you are a material type who can afford anything, you will only show her what maniac you are to look rich on the eyes of those around you.

If you have overleaped yourself she will notice it pretty soon and this will result in a failure. You will hardly have the possibility to take her every day to such elite places, so sooner or later everything will come to the fore. Therefore, it would be better to be yourself and to manifest your true abilities. You don't want to be liked for your money only, do you?

Naturally, it's not good to go to the other extreme, taking her to some common café to have a cup of mineral water for this will not impress her, anyway.

You are obliged to pay the bill. Be always prepared for this. A gentleman never leaves a woman to pay her bill. But if you have fallen onto some quite emancipated woman, who does not accept treats and insists on sharing the bill, you may still show some resentment, but reconcile in the end. If this will make her feel better, there's no problem to share the bill.

The best thing is to take her to dinner in some cozy place or to cocktails. Cocktails are an exquisite version, which you both will like. Good old cinema is classics and is also an option, but you should try to understand what films she likes, so as not to make her spend two hours watching something she doesn't like. This will make her transfer her irritation with the film on your person which won't be good.

Any options for having a pleasant time different from those above are also acceptable, if only you have an idea whether she likes them or not. Let it be theatre, opera, circus, walk, Luna Park, confectionary, carting track etc. Whatever it may be, if only you have made up your mind from your acquaintance so far what she would like. If your acquaintance is a new one, it would not be easy, but then you can rely on the classic dinner.

The real man never leaves a woman to decide where to date because if you ask her: "Where do you wish to go?" , this may really be of no importance to her or she may not wish to tell and then she will answer you: "Where you say, it's all the same to me". Her answer will leave you in full darkness, therefore, be sure to always have a plan in advance for the evening.

If she has agreed to go out with you, she most probably

doesn't like only your sense of humour, but your looks, too. However, this means that you must try to look perfect.

Women have what may be called an annoying habit to notice the smallest details. If you have not taken care of some part of your appearance, be sure that she will notice it. In contrast to men, women spot such things like an unsewn button, a spoiled shirt, muddy shoes, unattended nails, poorly shaven face and all such things I already mentioned.

To avoid impressing her in some of these ways, select suitable clothes, pay attention whether they are clean and ironed. It is needless to say that you should take a bath, shave yourself and smell pleasant. We already talked about scent and its importance, for smells remain very long in human memory, therefore, she will probably relate you for long with the scent of your perfume.

The best advice is to be you. Women can easily detect pretence which repels them. Be funny and interesting, but beware to not overplay and become artificial. Do not take pains to impress her by the things you have done and the places you have visited. Tell her about yourself, too, but without a note of boasting and self-emphasis.

Let dialogue does not turn into monologue during which you are telling something interesting (in your opinion) or laughing at your own jokes. Show interest for her. What she likes to do, where she likes to go and things like that. Take as a basis the way you got acquainted and starting from there ask her some question which implies more than a "Yes" or "No" answer. Both women and men like to have someone listening to them, so give the chance to tell you about herself.

As I mentioned already, every woman likes to hear that she looks good, that she is amusing and interesting, that she has beautiful eyes and so on, but everything with due measure. If, during the whole evening, you are telling her how unique she is, you'd sooner have the opposite effect. Therefore, be moderate; tell her that she looks wonderful yet in the beginning and from there on try to not overdo.

Do not touch too serious topics, on which you may have different opinions, which may bring up argue and, if you are too zealous, spoil the evening. Avoid talking about foreign policy, war, racial or religious discrimination and things like that.

It is true that if some topic is of great interest to you, you will be curious to know her opinion on it, but let this be left for the second date. During the first date it would be better if the conversation is light, amusing and funny – thus, the experience will leave a much more pleasant remembrance than if you have discussed some serious topic and have argued on it.

Do not touch as well too personal things. There are things about which one is not prepared to talk on a first date. And, if she answers some of your questions by: "It happened like that" or some other indefinite phrase, do not poke for details. Obviously, she has told you what she was prepared to tell.

Don't talk about your joint future either – anyhow, it's only your first date. If you ask her what name she wishes to give to your first child, she will most probably run away immediately.

Don't forget that the real man never complains. She has not come to hear how nasty your boss is. You can tell her how nasty he is by telling some funny story, so that it sounds amusing, but not make her a listener of your life woes.

Of course, there is another important thing – don't be silent. Awkward pauses are no good; they will make you both feel uncomfortable. Therefore, try to have a spare topic for conversation, but not a too banal one. Anyway, it is not presumed that you have to talk without end. If the pause is not awkward, but you have just stopped the talk to look at each other, then there could be nothing better.

If she shows interest to meet with you again, moreover on some particular day, then this means that she really intends to have a second meeting. Moreover, if you come to terms as to what you will be doing next time, the plan is already made and there is great chance for things to get along.

But, if you part by the indefinite: "We shall call each other", then there is a chance for this being a delicate refusal on her side to see you any more. But this might not be the case. Therefore, you may call her again, but not too soon, say, in a couple of days. If she is indefinite on the phone, too, then there is not much hope. But, if you observe all these principles, you will hardly get a refusal. There is no woman who does not like a well-looking and attended man, who knows how to amuse a woman on a date. In all cases, the first date is something very, very important – the second one depends on it.

HER SIGNALS SHOWING THAT SHE LIKES YOU

All men and women are unique and it is very hard to know what may be taking place in their heads. When you have a crash on some woman, you probably start thinking things like: "Does she like me?', "Is she keen on such type of men like me?" and other questions of this kind.

It would have been incredibly easy, if we could read what was on women's mind. Unfortunately, this is impossible, but women have a thousand signals aiming to show they like a given man. You probably wonder what these signals are. You have seen them pretty often, but you have hardly been aware they showed she liked you.

When you told something funny, have you noticed how

loudly and jovially your date is laughing? So, there is something. Women know how important men's confidence is and they feed it subconsciously, laughing at the jokes of the man they like.

In this way they show him that they are feeling good in his company and that they are having quite a good time with him. Next time, when you are on a date, pay attention if she starts laughing easily, no matter whether she is in company or with you alone. Then, chances are great that she is into you. But, don't experiment with dull jokes only to test her and see her reaction.

Besides, when a woman likes a man, she tries to be in contact with him as much as she can. Her methods may be different depending on the place you come in contact. For instance, she likes to sit or stand by you, joins in the common conversation when you are in it, tries to have a talk with you alone, shows interest for your tastes etc.

You have surely noticed how some girls are staring at you. If at some time you notice that she has stared in you having no particular reason to do it, this means that she merely wants to look at you. Which is a clue that she probably likes you, unless of course, this is not the day on which you have come with a new hair styling, because in this case she may be staring at you just on account of it. However, if there is nothing new or unusual in your looks, and her eyes are shining when she looks at you, you may be sure that she likes you.

You can also trust your friends' opinion. Quite often, things seem much clearer on the outside; therefore, try to ask the opinion of a friend, who has seen you together with the girl in question. If this friend is a woman, her forecast will be more accurate - yet women know each other better. If someone from her company drops a hint that she likes you, it might be really so. Only, do not pay any attention, if this someone is the plotter of the company.

On the overall, if she likes you, she would sooner be nice to you, responsive, helpful etc.

If you share that you are a fan of some rock band and in a couple of days you find out that she knows the band's history, chances are great that she has made the effort know it just on account of you.

The easiest thing to make out is flirt. Naturally, the ideas about flirt may be different, but as a whole there are some things which leave no doubt as to the matter – any hints and jokes with sexual meaning addressed to you, witty remarks etc.

When a woman likes you, it is very probable that she will try to show it to you by using various occasions to touch you. Here, however, you should be attentive because her attitude may be purely friendly and the fact that she has embraced you on your birthday may be nothing more than a friendly gesture. It is important what your relations are and what her touch is like – whether she tries to prolong the embrace, presses herself close to you or simply embraces you as an expression of friendship.

You will surely also have some inner intuition to know whether she likes you or not. When a man is really interested whether a woman likes him or not, his brains sets to work immediately and prove the answers to his question through observations and feelings.

If you attempt to understand whether she likes you, she will most probably read these attempts, which makes no bad - thus, if she is interested in you, your attempts will make her happy and will facilitate things.

This way or that, the best way to know whether she likes you is to show her that you have a crash on her.

Some men will be quick to say that in such case there is a danger of being rejected and this is far from being pleasant at all. It is right, there is always some risk. But this should not frighten you – if she does not like you, the reason is not in you.

Human emotions are a very complex matter and no one

could be claimed guilty that one person loves another, but the other one does not respond. There might be thousands of reasons for this such as another man or fear of commitment. Or there may be no specific reason, but just chemistry is lacking.

In any case, do not trust only one of the signs of which I spoke so far. It just won't be enough, there should be at least several of them. And if all of them are available, then, run quickly to her before someone else has outrun you.

You should know that however you try to know whether she likes you and however you worry about this question, there is no way to bypass it. Every relation starts with more or less uncertainty, inner torments and a hundred thousand questions which can be reduced to a single one: "Does she like me?" So, watch her signals and your inner feelings which may help you answer this question.

TECHNIQUES FOR SUCCESSFUL FLIRT

Can flirt be taught or each of us practices it as much as one can? It is true that, like anything else, flirt has its tricks which may be mastered if there is a wish and a little diligence.

You should choose the flirting site. The most frequent choice is a bar or a cafe. Food and drinks create more informal background and people are willing to communicate more freely. If, however, you should be in the office – choose the rest or coffee place.

Find an adequate topic for conversation. It is easiest, if you are in the office during the break; then, the topic is clear. Some more delicate situations are those in the lift, in the bar, or in the street. But don't give up. Start straight away by a compliment, such as "The rose colour suits you very much", "What beautiful shoes!" or "It is such a nice day, don't you think so?"

Be clear about what exactly you want – just a flirt or a sexual flirt. Take into account that women often may interpret a mere smile as an invitation for something more. Or vice versa – even a long flirting may not prompt them your wishes or intentions. Be clear to the limit, so that they may not be any misunderstanding.

In contrast to women, who usually are more confident about their looks, men are often anxious that they don't look well. Forget all prejudices and your flirt will be more successful. Have greater confidence. Actually, one never knows what exactly women like – know that they seem to like namely you.

The first step in flirting is to show your feelings and emotions for her. Pay her a compliment, point out her positive features. Make it in her presence before a friend of hers. This will flatter her for sure.

In flirt, actions, i.e. body language, mean more than words. Study data shows that 55% of the way you are perceived depends on your looks and body language, 38% - on how you talk and only 7% - on what you really say.

It would be good to reduce the distance between you. Get

a little bit closer to her. Stretch your body forward, this will excite her.

When you talk to her, apart from your closer body, reduce the distance as well by a lusty and clutching look at her. Look into her eyes all the time. Flicker more frequently at times or drop down your eyes with a mysterious smile. Pass your eyes over her body when you feel she is looking at you.

If you have observed all recommendations and have had flirt with the purpose of dating the lady in question – be sure that, if not today, then quite soon she will invite you to go out herself.

How Can You Know Whether You Feel Passion or Love

S ometimes, we, men, find it difficult to know whether we feel love or mere passion for some woman. We often confuse these two different terms and a serious emotional mish-mash appears of which there is no way out without hurting or being hurt.

It is only passion when:

- Her body is the only thing that interests you – Yet before knowing her name, you already imagine her naked and wonder what sex with her will be.

- You leave immediately after you have made sex – You have become an expert in finding excuses why you should go after sex.

- You want to be with her for the sake of sex only – It would mean nothing to you even if you have not exchanged a couple of words. You can easily spend a couple of days without hearing her, until the next time you feel need of bed gymnastics.

- She is your hot line – After you have had a good drink with your friends on Friday evening, you remember about her at one o'clock in the night for the purpose of purely nightly amusements.

- You don't care about what she talks. You find thousand excuses to not spend some time with her, unless you make sex, of course.

This is definitely the behaviour of a man who does not have any feelings. If some woman behaves like that with you, and you have feelings for her, withdraw as soon as possible. But if you are doing it to a woman who has feelings for you, then this will be very base and mean on your part. You know the saying that what goes around comes around, so, be careful if you have decided to play with the feelings of any woman whosoever.

I hope I have explained the situation with passion, now comes the turn of the basic principles of love

Love is when:

- When you see her, everything else disappears, hours pass like minutes when talking with her, you listen with interest when she tells you about her day.

- You are overwhelmed by the strange feeling that without her your life will be empty. You start sharing with an increasing number of people that she is the woman for you; you even look through the rings at the jewelry. You would like to cry her name out before the whole world.

- You like her without make up or when her hair is wild. You want to spend your time with her only. The only thing you want is to be with her, no matter whether you will make sex or not.

- Even if she tells you that you'll have to wait for sex, you don't care because being with her is enough for you.

- It becomes very important to you for your parents to like her and to be together at each family event. No matter whether you are walking your dog or going out with friends, you want her to be with you.

- You want so much to be all the time with her that you

dream how you could be together at work. But since this cannot happen, you call her twice a day to tell her you are thinking of her.

– Suddenly, you start liking romantic films, as well as romantic songs. While you are listening to them, you are thinking of her. You send her flowers with romantic card and prepare on your own dinner for two, put on a new table-cloth and light candles.

– You spoil for a fight every time somebody says something bad about her. Besides, in public places, you agree with everything she says, no matter your opinion on the issue is.

You also want to be a better man for her and you want to change. She makes you happy and you would do anything to make her happy, too.

How to Treat Beautiful Women

Men like to be tortured by women, especially by beautiful ones. When a man does anything for a woman, she often gets out of hand and starts behaving rude.

When a woman starts behaving like this, this is a warning sign. She is not delicate and demonstrates poor breeding. In spite of it all, you will call her again, moreover, three days later. After such an indelicate behaviour on her part, you should not call her at least two weeks – if at all, it deserves calling her again.

During your conversation you should have mentioned that you have felt repulsed. You may drop a hint like: "How many people will we be on our next date? Will you bring your granny this time to introduce me to her?"

One cannot imagine the follies a man can do for a beautiful woman. But does it pay to let her play with you the way she likes. The real man has pride.

If he doesn't like anything in a woman, then he simply stops contacts with her. He never wastes his time with a woman who thinks that world goes round her. You are a real man and you are not the type of man he can mock at. When you don't like something, tell her and withdraw.

This is the only way only you to stand out on her eyes because you will show self-respect and pride.

On the other hand, if you don't like something in her behaviour and you tell it to her immediately and give her up, this may attract her strongly because in this way you will show what a strong man you are. However smart she is, you don't like her character and you leave her.

Besides, this may arouse her interest and she may start hunting for you. She will pay excuses and she will promise that she will be different on your next date. It depends on you whether you will give her another chance. One can hardly change. Ask yourself does it pay to bother about such a woman.

It seems all men are in her feet and she thinks she thinks she can play the boss with anyone. And when you withdraw, you become immediately an object of desire for her. It seems everything is too easy for her and since you become inaccessible to her, this kindles her interest for you. Ask yourself if it pays to be with such a heartless woman. My advice is to not bother, however beautiful she is.

How Can You Ask Her Phone Number

Many men prefer to sit at home on weekends, to drink with friends, to scratch their abdomen and just be lazy just because there is nobody on the love horizon.

The only problem of many of them is that they do not know where to start a hit-on from. After all, this is not that difficult, since there are milliards of people on the Earth. Usually, everything starts by taking her phone number.

Before asking the girl's number, you should start a conversation with her. Don't forget that many before you are sure to have also asked her number, so try to be a little bit more ingenuous. Talk to her about something funny, keep an amusing conversation. Don't forget that this is not science and there are no strict written rules. Be amusing or a bit shy, but most important, be yourself.

There is one reliable method I have tried myself. I was

burning with shame to ask the phone number of a girl, and I had only one minute because her bus was coming. I had to shoot, but I didn't want it to be that simple. Therefore, I forged in a hurry: "Sorry, but you seem to me a lucky girl, and I wonder whether I will not have a chance, if I do the pools using the digits of your phone number". It is true that I did not do the pools afterwards, but I won some very nice moments with her.

The main rule says that when you get the phone number of some girl, you should act with her until you understand whether it pays and whether anything will come of it.

The idea to collect 20 phone numbers in one evening will at the worst take you to the confusion who was who and in the end you will not even know with whom you talking on the phone. You can guess yourself that this leads to failure. Just that, concentrate on one girl.

When you manage to get her phone number, remember the following rule: one message, two calls, and three days.

If she does not pick up and you start filling up her voice mail with messages and vain calls you risk her taking you for a psycho or for a man awfully depressed by loneliness.

During your first conversation make a good presentation of you. It is important to succeed to carry out an easy conversation which will be amusing for her.

In the end you may invite her on a date depending on whether you were successful in cheering her up or intriguing her.

During your first conversation it is advisable to not talk on some topics, such as former partners. It is the same as when, during a work interview, you start talking about how bad it was with your former employer. Moreover, in this way you will only show her how you will talk about her, too, some day when you break off, if your relationships come to a relation at all.

Putting it briefly, if you want to take the phone number of some girl, do it with confidence, be sure of yourself that she will not repulse you, because if you ask it and look unconfident, she will feel it and things may not get on. Be amusing and ingenuous in what you are telling her. Then enjoy the date and try to make it so that another one follows.

How to Get to Her When She Is in Her Friends' Company

You have surely happened to like a girl who is surrounded by the company of her friends who wouldn't let her to contact with you or sooner, wouldn't let you to come closer.

It is really complicated when you are in a bar or a club and the girl you like is surrounded by her perpetual friends. In such case you surely give it up quite soon though you'd like very much to talk to her.

Well, but if this girl is the woman of your life, but because of her annoying friends you anyway don't succeed to make contact with her? Is it worth giving up? So, take a deep breath and act.

You take one of your friends who can amuse her friends while you are doing your best to impress her. Moreover, your friend may do so as to raise high your reputation. If he goes there first and starts talking with some of the girls, he might as soon mention something positive about you.

Besides, he can ask some things about her and understand whether she is occupied etc. After he has explored the ground, he may ask you to join them and introduce you to the girls with whom he is already acquainted. Thus, while he is telling amusing stories to the rest, you will have enough time to talk with her.

You should only take care that this friend of yours is not some plotter or a man who envies you and is glad at each failure of yours. It would be best if he is married or has a girlfriend. Thus, he will not have the chance to fool you or to have the same goal as you. So, the action plan is perfect when you trust completely your friend and know that he will not do anything to discredit you.

If you act using such an honest and faithful friend, then you surely will stand out and strike oil.

But if you don't have such friends who you may trust for such a mission, then you should act on yourself. You will be definitely a hero on the eyes of all your companions, because you will make your way into a hard territory, moreover all alone.

You should have a delicate approach. Let her know that it is for her you are getting into their company. This will definitely be very easy when you establish eye contact with her. In this way you will let her know as well as her friends, that all this is on account of her.

If the place is very noisy, stay close to her and bend slightly to her ear. Tell her something funny, try to amuse her. If she continues to behave distant, ignore her for a while and then attack again. If she still behaves distant, focus on someone else.

But if she smiles and you feel that she is pleased to be in your company, then you should pull her out of her friends. This will be somewhat difficult because there surely will be a friend to envy her that she is the only object of interest. So, they will try to fool you, but you don't give up and be good and kind with everybody. Be patient for if she's really interested she'll arrange it so as to get rid for a while of her friends. When you are alone it is the time to present yourself as good as possible, to treat her to a drink, to make her a compliment, in short, to show your great interest for her.

When she says it's time to go, take her phone number and

offer her to drive her home. If you wish things between you to go deeper, you shouldn't show her anyhow that you want to go to bed right now.

But if you wish to take her to bed for this evening only, it is another thing. Invite her to your place and if she accepts, this means you are successful. But if she gives you a brush-off, focus on some other girl who is standing a little bit apart of the crowd. Thus, the chance to start a conversation, to get closer, and in the end, to finish at your place, is much greater.

Just don't think that girls standing apart are any losers. On the contrary – it is namely these who have gone out "hunting". And in the case, the role of prey for you is more than attractive.

After you have started talking with her and piled her with compliments, it is time to take her to your place. Offer her something that looks quite spontaneous.

The classical "I've got a bottle of wine at home, we may continue our talk there" works in most cases because it suggests a fun follow-up, moreover the idea of a man having an unopened bottle of wine in his fridge looks strongly exciting on women's eyes.

You are probably curious to know how she will manage in bed. Is she good? Are there any clues showing whether a woman is naughty in bed?

One of the main things is the presence of confidence. If she has strongly pronounced confidence based on her looks and not on her professional or intellectual abilities, this means that she would try new tricks in bed.

Moreover, women who do not refuse, often have more possibilities to exercise. Just as you succeeded to take her to your place, obviously, anyone else in the bar has had the same chance. If she regularly ends the evening with unknown men in their places, this means definitely that she has great experience.

There is also another case, if she talks all the time how good she is and how she can do some things that other women can't do, then, it may turn out that she has no experience at all. Women who boast too much in the sexual aspect, in most cases are simply overplaying.

Another basic method to see whether she is good in sex is to kiss her. If you like the way she kisses, this means that you will match in bed. Also, if she is flexible and can dance well. Her sexy movements, the bends of her body might be an indicator of her skills in the horizontal position.

And if she practices regularly dances, yoga, aerobics or is a ballet-dancer, then the situation is more than clear. The fact that she exercises some sport and maintains good physical shape may be also a proof that you will not get bored in bed with her. The fact that she has a beautiful body and she knows it, that she is self-confident and is not ashamed of anything is also quite indicative that she will be perfect in sex. Her tight bottom, her strong thighs, her endurance and the poses she knows will make you exclusively happy.

If she invites you to her place and plays some quiet and nice music or lights aromatic candles and turns off the light. Begins touching you or responds to your attempts for physical contact, then she is trying to release tension as soon as possible and to get intimate with you. This means that she loves sex and she is ready to do everything to have a good time and this, on the other part, shows that she knows how and that she has experience.

Chances are that she may be good on massage and, obviously, with the right techniques. Or she may love to pamper her body visiting spa centres. These are also well manifested signs of a woman who is capable and who is not ashamed to show her skills.

Things You Should Never Tell Her after Sex

After you have already succeeded to take her to bed you must be careful what to say after sex, because there are things that may offend her very much.

The sex has been great. After which you have blurted out something so wrong that the woman next to you has pulled on her clothes with the utmost speed, dashed out and still goes to the opposite sidewalk when you meet in the street. What are these wrong statements?

If you tell something like: "I felt very good! Just like with my ex."

"I must leave right now. No, I don't have time for hugs now."

"I bet you have not done such things with your ex in bed."

"I was thinking something about my work. No, I didn't want to say I was thinking this while we had sex! Really!"

"Alex told me how once they tried an interesting pose with his friend. Don't you think that you should experiment a little bit more? Not that I don't feel good this way."

"We feel so good together! If only my mother liked you, too."

"How about this pretty friend of yours – Would she not agree to make a three?"

"What you did to me was really great, but maybe you should exercise more."

"Does it seem to me like that or you have really gained weight?"

"I am so tired. Can you turn off the lamp, pick up my socks from the floor and cover me up? Oh, and set the alarm clock for tomorrow morning and keep quiet because I am already going to sleep."

"I am not accustomed to sleep by someone, so, you guess what... don't be angry."

"Mmm, it was great… will you call a taxi or shall I do it?"

"It was super, if you do the same thing to me the next time, I may decide to date you seriously."

And other things like that which, even you want her only for the night, you should never tell her.

How Could You Know that the Woman You Like Is Just Using You?

t may turn out that the woman you do everything for is just using you and gets amused on account of this. But love is blind and we cannot always realize on time that we are being used only to satisfy someone's whims without any reason for that. Such are the cases when:

Yet on the second date she proposes moving to your place since her rent is very high or she is fed up with living with her parents/roommates or some reason like that. After which she says it is quite natural that you should go on paying for water, electricity and other bills because the home is yours after all.

And what does she do on your first date since on your second one she already wants to move to your place? She pumps you about the condition of your bank account, the size of your home, the brand of your car. If she understands that you have none of the above-mentioned things, her charming sense of humour, her good mood and her playful look become easily downcast and her eyes start wandering about the place in search for a more solvent candidate.

Her calls are expressed in: "Hi, I need help" or "Hi, I need you urgently". She never sounds like: "Hi, I only wanted to hear you and to tell you that I love you."

She never expresses a wish to share the bill, to give you a treat or to cook something at your place. She insists on going to expensive places, because it is better there. She thinks that it is quite normal for you to take care of her and her whims. She also thinks that common bars and pubs are below her level. She likes places where they offer her favourite things – black caviar, salmon and 12-year-old whisky.

She wants you to go shopping for clothes with her where she chooses and you pay. She sends you the bills from the beauty and spa saloons – after all, she is making herself beautiful for you.

She has liked an airplane excursion to Spain and dramatically declares that she doesn't want anything else for her birthday.

She invites to dinner in your name all her friends and reserves a table in the restaurant of a five-star hotel. And when you drop a hint that you're not a bank and that she goes a little bit too far, she starts crying and tells you don't love her.

WHEN TO TELL A WOMAN YOU LOVE HER

It is true that women long to hear the cherished words "I love you", pronounced, if possible, by the man of their dreams, moreover with soft, tender and sincere voice.

The truth is that women do not jump with joy every time they here this. It is true that sometime they would "kill a man" just to hear it from us, men, but some other time they would sooner kill us, if we blurt it out in inappropriate time or place or for the fourth time in a row within half an hour.

This is the first problem, when we tell it too often. It is true that they are glad to hear it, but if we are telling it continuously in the form of sms or e-mail, there comes a time when they seize paying attention to it. Then, the beautiful words "I love you" will turn into something like "Hello" and will not delight them at all.

The other problem is if you do not hit the appropriate time. Sometimes even women are not in the tune for confessions. Therefore, if you blurt out an "I love you" when they have quite different, moreover, serious problems, you will accumulate more negative score than would a woman if she turns off the TV while you are watching the Champion League final.

They would not be glad as well to hear the magic words if they are not sincere. Women really have something like an intuition and easily detect false, especially when it comes to feelings. Therefore, don't lie to them. A woman would prefer telling her frankly what you really like in her (be it even a single thing and something of the sort "I like to make sex") than telling her how unique she is and how you love her more than anything else while you don't mean it, actually.

Nearly any woman will doubt your insincere confession and you will win nothing as a result of it.

And last, if you are really in love with this woman and you want to tell her "I love you", but if you, anyhow, cannot do it? Then there is no problem. If you have decided that you want to tell it to her, just do it. Take her on a date, be yourself, and make her the relevant confession, not worrying about anything. If you are sincere, your girl will appreciate it and your confession really, but absolutely really will make feel in the seventh heaven.

WHY WOMEN GIVE MEN A BRUSH-OFF?

Which is our greatest problem when a woman brushes us off? You go and tell her that you like her. You inform her and you expect her reaction. If it is positive, you are pleased, but if she brushes you off you feel like the greatest fool on Earth and for a moment you'd like to be a mouse, so that you can hide in the most secret hole.

This is only one of the several big mistakes we make. It is not good to be hasty. If you have known her for several months and you are dating all the time and you buy her a present telling her that you feel something more than affection for her, this is good.

But if you have gone out only a couple of times and you make her a confession, it is almost certain that you will not be satisfied with her reaction.

As you already understood, women like the manly type of men, who alone controls the situations around him. Therefore, it would be silly to lend a back to her and to agree with everything she says and wants. You remember that the manly type looks as if it is surrounded all the time with beautiful women and if a woman wants to win him, it is her that should lend her back for him and not vice versa.

If you don't behave this way you will not only lose the battle, but you will discredit yourself. Women do not approve such behaviour.

We talked about how good it is for you to be confident, but if you turn into an annoying bore who begs her compliments, then this shows only how unconfident you are and such an attitude will not have good results for you.

If your questions also reveal uncertainty, then it is almost sure that she will repel you. Such as, for instance: "What cinema centre shall we go to – in the mall or in the centre?" Such questions sound to a woman like: "I am not sure whether you will like the cinema at the mall, that's why I am asking you where exactly you want to go" and this alone shows how timid and unconfident you are. But, as you understood, unconfident is equal to nothing.

But, if you display just the opposite behaviour, if always you are the leading one, if you surprise her and give her unexpected presents, then you will surely have only positive score. So, take her to unknown places, be different, surprise her with everything, have control on everything and make so that she can have such a memorable time with you only. And from now on she will be unable to do without these memorable moments; therefore, she won't be able to tear herself away from you.

Be as well a little mysterious and don't reveal everything about you. Do not respond every time she wants you to meet. Naturally, she must be aware that you feel good when you are together, but that you can't be all the time with her because your life does not go round her only.

You may go to play football with friends, or to fitness or you may think of some other occupations thereby showing her that you can spend your time well without her, either. You are happy with her, but your life was happy before she appeared, too.

Do never behave like a mouse with her. This means talking to her in an uncertain voice or making such gestures and mimics which will only show that you are not confident and assured of you. You are a man and you must be confident showing this with all your movements. Your body language should be manly which means no womanly bends, gates etc. Your body must emit composure, no abrupt or hasty movements. You body must emit: "I feel well in my skin, I like myself, I feel comfortable and nothing and nobody can make me feel bad."

Women like to be in the company of men they feel interesting with, simply because they find it funny to spend their time with them.

Naturally, they should be also attracted by your looks. The looks of a loser are something desperate for every man. If you are slim and tall you should be careful because such men often have a funny and easily turning into what appears to be "loser's" gate.

I mentioned already about the gestures. It would be best without any gestures. Thrust your hands into your pockets.

If you wear glasses, you may put contact lenses. Thus, you will even be able to change the colour of your eyes. If you have black hair, you may take blue lenses which will make you much more attractive. Of course, you must try because everyone looks different. And if you don't want to put on contact lenses, keep your glasses. But, be thoughtful and moony. Thus you will look intelligent and very cute.

Your look must be cheeky, frowning and provocative. The other extreme is moony and thoughtful. Everything else is loser's way.

Don't talk much, answer briefly and clearly. Don't fall in details, be mysterious.

How to Start a
Successful Talk
with an Unknown
Woman

tarting a talk with a beautiful woman may appear to be an exclusively nervous experience. Many men are so frightened by attractive women that they try to avoid those of them whom they do not know and thus every day they miss the opportunity of getting acquainted with smart women. Here is one explanation as to why beautiful women are often unhappy and lonely.

The truth is that who plays, he wins – regardless of what happens. Most men are too much absorbed by the thought whether the talk is going well and whether they will leave with her phone number. This is an enormous mistake. When you have approached her and talked to her you have made 95% of what the other men may only dream of. Be proud of what you have achieved – whatever it happens you are one step before the rest with this courage of yours. After you have made the first decisive move, you may relax and enjoy the conversation with her.

Learn to turn your fear into your friend. Next time you became anxious to tell something to a woman think that actually, fear is a sign that you should do something. Thus, you will become more confident and you will meet more women. You will be pleased, as well as women, that anyhow, there are some decisive and courageous men left.

And can you explain exactly the word "courage"? Actually, this is "the ability to undertake an action regardless of fear, regardless of consequences". The heroes from the films are always courageous because they are always ready to fight despite the risk of death. In this case, you become a hero as well because you approach her and talk to her despite the risk of rejection.

The next time you want to talk with a woman and you feel that your palms are sweating with anxiety, take it as a chance to overcome your fear. You will feel how your self-confidence will boost afterwards and you won't be asking yourself questions like: "What would have happened if I had had the courage to talk to her?"

Naturally, when you talk to a woman she would sometimes behave awfully and will pout at each word of yours. Yes, but this may be an exception. It doesn't mean that all women will behave like that. Don't take it into your head that all women behave pompously because this is really far from the truth.

One of the best ways to go to the woman you like is to learn to ignore the excuses you figure out yourself: "She will never pay attention to me", "She is obviously busy and I wouldn't like to interrupt her", "Maybe she has a boyfriend". All these excuses come from your desire to stay in your "safety area" and each of them is mere nonsense. As soon as you are overwhelmed by such thoughts, head forward to get acquainted with her. The more often you do it with different women, the more confident you will become. Even if you are not lucky some time, be glad that you have taken the initiative. Quite a few men would have your courage, so you are showing strength while they remain weaklings.

Stop trying to imagine what you should say and simply head forward to her. Yet on the way you'll find something to impress you of which it may be worth talking with her. Use it, no matter how common it may seem to you. The key to success is to start the conversation. Then, everything becomes easier and will arrange by itself.

THE THINGS THAT
WILL IMPRESS HER

I f you want to really impress the woman you like, you should apply some effort. A lot of men think that to impress a woman it is enough to open a bottle of champagne, to play good music and to light candles. But, if you want to go soon to bed with her you need to make another kind of impression.

When you are at a restaurant with her and someone calls you on the mobile when licking it up you'd better say: "I'm busy with a very pleasant person right now and I would ask you to call me tomorrow". This will make her feel very special. You can also make a friend of yours call you right then and warn him that you will be talking in this way so as to impress her.

After that you may switch off your mobile before her and tell her that you don't want to lose a second of the magnificent time spent with her. This will show her that you feel wonderful in her company, you are ready to pay all your attention to her and that she is the most important for you at this moment.

When you chat online you'd better answer immediately her messages. If you are late, she will think you are chatting with other women too and this will change immediately her attitude for you. You should as well not answer by one sentence for this will mean that you are not willing to talk with her. If she asks you: "How was your day?" you may tell her in detail what has happened.

Talk about books and films. Tell her what your favourite film is about and she will tell you about her preferences as well. Thus, she will feel you closer and she will be very pleased that you have spent time on her and have told her what impresses you. The same holds for books. You will make her an exclusively good impression if it turns out that you have read one and the same book. This will reveal your intelligence to her and women are greatly impressed by clever men.

Introduce her to your friends and talk good about her before them. Thus, you will show to them and to her that you are proud to go out with such a woman. And this may only flatter her. The same holds for compliments. You can tell her how beautiful she is not only when you are alone, but also before your friends as well as before her friends. You will notice immediately the smile on her face and you are sure to win a positive score.

Always use the words "Thank you" and "You are welcome",

which will show your good manners. People who don't have good manners don't use such words.

Talk with respect about others. Never accuse them of anything before her. You may do it avoiding negative comments, which may offend someone. This will show her that you are sensible and that you don't need to humiliate others, so that you may stand out.

There is one thing which will always impress women. Always open the door to everyone who follows you near, not to her only. This will definitely show that you are well-bred and have good manners.

Never interrupt her and wait until she tells what she wants after which you may start speaking. She might be very offended if you interrupt her because this shows lack of respect for what she says.

Never chew while you are talking with her on the phone because this produces sounds which are not pleasant to her ear. And don't forget to disable your mobile in the cinema, theatre etc.

Send her flowers when she is at work. Thus all her colleagues will know that there is someone who values her and this will make her happy.

Signs Showing That You Should Not Waste Your Time with Her

If she tells you that she is not ready for a serious relation. Women often tell it when they are not interested in somebody. If she tells you that she is not ready for a relation with you, this means that she does not see in you potential for serious relation. She may think that the car you drive is not enough luxurious for her. If such a thing happens to you, be glad that you have not lost your time with her.

Another sign is if she does not laugh at your jokes. To women, laughter is kind of flirting. If she liked you, she would have laughed even if she did not understand your joke or if you were a poor joke-teller because thus she would show her interest.

If you call her and she does not answer your calls. She may pretend to be inaccessible, but if you call her several more times and she does not lift the receiver, this means that she has definitely no interest. In this case, there is no sense to call her any more. But you should necessarily try to contact her at least three times because there are many books advising women to hold back in the beginning and to pretend to be inaccessible.

If she cancels your meetings all the time, then she is definitely not willing to meet you. Remember that, if a woman likes you, she will turn the word upside down to find a way to meet you.

If she avoids eye contact and physical intimacy this also shows that things will not come to be. If the woman is impressed by you, she will naturally want to be close to you.

Moreover, if she talks before you about other men, she obviously feels you as her girl friend and simply shares her feelings. She always talks about someone else or shares some stories about him. Or she tries to make contact between you and some of her friends.

She doesn't want to kiss you in public. There are many women who have a problem with this and you should not worry if everything is OK when you are alone. But, if she does not want to kiss you then too, this is already another case.

If she doesn't let you to stay alone in her place and she doesn't want to give you the key. It may be that there are some things in the flat that she is not ready to show you. But if you have been dating for two years and things continue this way, probably there is really something wrong that she is hiding.

If she has many male friends and goes out with them all the time. This is not quite a sign. Some women simply have a lot of male friends, but anyhow it would be advisable to give an eye to it. But if she flirts with men before you, this is definitely a sign.

If she is not dressed sexy and does not attempt to attract male attention. If a woman looks for a partner she would have dressed up. But if she has not dressed up, she would probably not answer your tease, because she doesn't feel attractive and she will give you a brush-off.

A man can also guess from some hints whether the chick is seeking a partner for the evening at all. The correct choice of a girl depends totally on visual hints. If you are in a club and you try all chicks in turn this will not be good for you because everyone will conclude that you are the successive Don Juan. Then, most probably, women will give you immediately a brush-off. If you are in a bar, you'd better try on no more than two women. But if you are invited to a party, you can afford a couple of successive attempts there because at such an event it is natural for a man to start a conversation with many unknown people.

If it makes you an impression that the woman you have leveled yourself at seems depressed or that she'd rather peck than talk friendly with people, then you may be have a chance to get to sex, but you should anyhow be careful with the way you approach her because she may soon drive you away. Be gentle in the beginning and tell her something funny, may be you are the one to cheer her up. Afterwards you may act because such depressed and hostile women easily surrender to men.

If she frowns at your sexual hints and looks virtuous on the overall, you'll probably not be lucky. But on the other hand, if, notwithstanding the mistake with the sexual hint, she maintains a friendly conversation with you, you might have fallen upon a more conservative woman, who simply expects you to change your approach for her.

Sometimes women pretend that they do not understand the attempts to hit on them just for the purpose of enjoying longer the man's attention. If, even upon a bare hint on your part, you get the impression that she behaves with you as if you are some of her friends, but she is still gentle, maybe her purpose is simply to make you give up your sexual intentions, but she hopes that you will continue to manifest your friendly attitude. But if you keep on with your hints, she might become sick with it and she may discard you quite rudely.

Some women are just mean. They like to bully men and they find it normal. Anyone who has ventured to stay in front of them risks being eaten with his clothes. The guilt will not be yours but the bitch's who is interested in nobody but herself.

Or if she is harsh with you or starts crying at you, she might be checking up how far you may stand family scenes. Polite people do not treat a stranger as if they have known each other for a hundred years and are fed up with each other. Therefore, discard her at once.

Chances are that the woman you like is not in good mood. You are doing the utmost, but things are not getting anyhow. You are convinced that you have played your trump-cards in the right order, but anyhow, there is no effect. She may be indisposed or she may not have a good day. Anyhow, if there are no clear signs that she finds you too nasty, you may proceed delicately and on some other day you may be successful.

There is another case when she wants to drive you away; then, she would mention the word "boyfriend", "husband", "marriage" or "relation" yet during the first minutes of the conversation. Some women would even use the hit-on as a chance to test how serious the man is towards the relation. This means that she gives a signal that she would not waste her time in nonchalant flirting, unless she sees potential for serious relation, which is in absolute contrast with the intentions of the serial lover. Even when this is the sexiest chick at the party who makes you revise your intention to hit on chicks for pleasure, remember that a woman who lays down such serious terms so hastily is a person who wishes to stand in the lead even at this quite early stage.

And there may be one who would ignore your questions so that you'll have to repeat them more than once. Or she would answer you by "Yes" or "No", applying no effort to maintain dialogue. This also points to lack of interest.

And if you have been talking for some time, everything seems normal but when you suddenly touch her hand or establish a similar physical contact, she apparently draws herself away, not trying to conceal it. This might be a sign that you have gone beyond the bounds unauthorized.

And if she is wearing an engagement ring, this looks quite discouraging in itself, but one never knows because she might be simply pretending. Some women use the ring to filter the serious candidates out of their way.

Many of the engaged or married women or women with low

self-esteem attempt to prove to themselves that men still like them. Therefore, they flirt with you having no intention to go further. They are not interested in your personality, but in getting you excited. And when such a woman makes sure that you are interested in her she would feel relieved that she is still worth for, and will give you up.

But she might be occupied, having a boyfriend or a spouse whom she values greatly. Here, you have no right to be angry, but you may only be happy that there are still such people that are so faithful to each other. But before trying to hit on some woman, you'd better make sure she is not engaged to avoid being given a brush-off.

And if you hear something like: "I want to take a pause in dating men" or "I need some time to put my life in order", it means that she has just ended a relation and she is simply not in the mood for a new one. Anyhow, you may become only her friend and attack again when she recovers from her depression.

First of all you should know that even if you are the perfect man in everything, women may not always like you. Every person is different and likes different thing. You may be manly, intelligent, handsome, and rich but a woman may still not like you. Everything is a matter of taste. I know beautiful women who are into quite unattractive men. But this does not mean that you should not keep my advice as to behaviour, maintenance etc. First f all, be yourself and don't worry if some woman discards you. If you have good looks, dress well, if you can be amusing and interesting and the woman you like still has no interest for you, it means that the problem is mainly in her. Your confidence should not drop, on the contrary – you are free and you can try with any other woman. Don't let a woman's discarding disappoint you. Remember that it happens to the best ones, either.

After you become more skilled in the art of talking to a woman, you will find it easier to know what hints mean what. But if you fall in some of the above situations, take decision and get away.

Is It True That Women Like Only Men with Much Money?

You are definitely sure that the thing women like most in a man is money. But this is part true and part not true.

Most men imagine a date with a girl in the following way: you pick her up from her place, take her somewhere (café, cinema, restaurant, disco etc.), you are at the appropriate place, then you take her home. Probably, you think that women reason the same way.

But the truth is that there are different types of women. And if you have fallen upon someone who has undoubtedly shown you that you are the only man for her as soon as your pocket is full and open for her, then it is normal to think that all women are like that.

It is true that all women like men to take care of them. But this is quite a normal feature of woman's nature. Even what is called a tough girl needs someone to take care of her, to amuse her, if she is gloomy, to help her change the light bulb, to attend to her when she is ill etc. Each woman who says she doesn't need a man is either lying or doesn't know yet what she wants.

The practice for the man to pay the bill is still modern. There is so much tradition, history and habit in it and it is not going to change soon. As you already learned, at least during the first several meetings it is obligatory for you to pay the bill even if she wants to share it.

After several meetings, she herself would feel uneasy with only you paying the bills therefore, she will propose to share it this time and now you may already accept. Naturally, if she is not of the type of women I mentioned before.

However, you may still wonder how important it is for the woman whether you are a businessman with a luxurious car or an unemployed man who can't still find a work he deserves?

The truth is that money matters and this is normal. But this does not mean at all that you should be a businessman in order to conquer her. Money really is not everything, however banal this may sound. But if you are jobless, you'll hardly have a chance. No woman will stand by you, if you spend your days in encircling to no use job ads in the newspaper and explaining that "you'd like very much to take her somewhere, to pamper her, but now you are just having a difficult moment". There are difficult moments and nobody is insured against them. The problem is to recover as soon as possible and to find a way out of the situation. If only you are willing, will anyhow find some work which you like and which brings you the needed funds.

TRANSLATION OF THE MOST POPULAR KEY WOMEN'S PHRASES

Sometimes women tell us something, but at the same time they want to tell something else or attempt to conceal something in this way. Here are some of the most noble women lies and key phrases:

I like you, but I don't want to ruin our friendship:

Translation

You don't mean anything to me. Forget about dating me. And don't ever, really never try again. You've got no chances, so cut down all hopes.

What would you say if we give us some rest and reconsider things between us?

106

Translation

It was wonderful in the beginning, but I do not feel this passion any more. The thrill died long ago and I am staying with you just because I don't want to hurt you. But since I'm not happy, I can't stand you any more. We'd better part.

I have had quite few men before you, but you are the best!

Translation

I know how sensitive you are on the topic "How do I play in bed?" Take it easy – I am quite patient and devoted and if there is something you may learn, I will be happy to show it to you. You should only listen carefully to me and you will really be the best.

The present doesn't matter, the gesture matters!

Translation

Nonsense! Naturally, I prefer a jewel to a vacuum-cleaner and a dress to a pan.

Do you find this one beautiful?

Translation

You don't find this one is more beautiful than me? Even if she is, don't even think of saying it!

No matter that today is three years since we started dating. You may sit quiet and watch the World Final, while I am making a salad for you.

Translation

Anyway, we are more important than anything – sports, car, parents etc. If you remember this rule, our relation is going to last very long.

Naturally, that I don't mind your parents coming.

Translation

If only they call one month in advance and stay a little. There is nothing more hazardous than a mother-in-law at home. Anyway, we alone know how to clean our house and how to look after the children.

Do you really want us to go to this place?

Translation

I prefer staying at home and looking at my favourite series instead of dragging myself to that dull meeting with your dull and boring colleagues and friends from your dull work.

Are you going to put on this?

Translation

Change your clothes immediately before someone has seen you and I died of shame.

You've got no belly. Really!

Translation

I am tactful. Even if I ask you whether I have put on weight, I expect you to say "No!". Therefore, I am answering you the same way. But if you really notice you have put on weight, it would be good to take measures on time, not only for me, but for your own self. So – less beer and more walking.

Do you think that my bottom looks big?

Translation

Tell me that my bottom looks great, that you can't take your eyes off it and you get erection only by looking at it.

Of course, I cummed!

Translation

If I have decided to let you in, but I haven't cummed, I happen to lie at times. Not because you aren't good, but just because I'm sleepy or my head is full with all sorts of other things, and the only thing I need is peace. But if I tell you the truth, I know I will not have it because you will either start asking questions or will start working on the problem.

I've got a headache!

Translation

The most trivial, but often used lie, when I don't want to make sex. I am not a sex-machine, after all. There are days when sex is my last concern. Anyway, it is me who decides whether I want it or not. So, don't insist, but think of something else – we could watch a film, for instance.

The dress costs 15$.

Translation

I dropped a zero, at that in the end. But, just look at it – pink and sexy. If it's no problem for a man to go all the winter round in two pullovers, this does not mean that women can do the same. We have genetic predisposition to want more clothes. And just look around – how many shops for women's clothes. How could I not fall into temptation?

Where have you been?

Translation

Why are you so late? Now, start fawning on me and lending your back on me.

I had dinner with a she-colleague.

Translation

But, she was of the male sex. Quite often you are saving info about colleagues, fellow-students, friends when they are of the opposite sex. Not because there is something between us, but just for the simple reason that I don't feel like explaining for an hour what is his name, how does he look, what car he drives, does he attract me and piles of other questions you overwhelm me with.

Oh, do you know this person?

Translation

Have you slept with this bitch?

Are you dating with somebody now?

Translation

How fast can you break-off with your current friend?

How Can You Dominate Women and Take Them to Bed?

The first thing you should do is to understand what it means to be a man. You have some wishes, emotions etc. Don't be ashamed of them. Don't be ashamed of your wishes to be intimate or to make sex with many women. There's nothing shameful in being a man.

As a man, you must be strong, not physically, but at will. Never accept rude behaviour from others, women in the least. If a woman does something you don't like, tell her. Don't be rude, be composed, but resolute. Don't let woman take the lead of you, never do what they want or ask you to do. Do only what you want and leave them to either agree with you or leave. You should be uncompromising. This is the price of success.

Don't find excuses for your wishes or actions.

Do as much as you can to improve your looks, as I already told. Clothes, shoes (very important), get shaved, no hair on your body, teeth, hair styling, nails, be clean, buy good eau de Cologne, even if should pay a bit too much for it. This is very important. Seek a woman's advice, if necessary.

You should practice. Think of a phrase to start a conversation with. Example: I noticed you when I was entering/passing by and had to spare a second to find out what you are like...

Then, start a brief talk. Don't give out compliments for a woman's beauty; they are hearing it all the time, especially if they are really very beautiful. Or if you give some, you should at least be very skilled and almost indifferent and, as I said before, be ingenious. You need to practice, 10-12 girls a day, 4-5 times a week. THIS IS VERY IMPORTANT: Body language. Walk always straight, shoulders drawn back, head lifted up, chest forward. Behave as a nut, make slow, calculated movements, wink your eyes slowly, speak slowly, pausing between sentences and words. (Not that much to look funny. The idea is to show you feel so comfortable in your body that it even gives you a pain). When you see a girl, look her straight into the eyes. Never drop your eyes off her before she has done it. Thus, you show her who is stronger.

Be composed, even indifferent. Don't give it up much that you want a woman because they always want to have a challenge and not someone whom they may have without much pain. This holds for everything you make with women.
Be dominating, don't hide your sexual wants (this is done by touching and body language, not by words, though it is good to use sexual overtones where appropriate, i.e. when the conversation allows it.)

Don't be afraid to trifle with girls. For instance, if someone is on high heels tell her: What's the matter about these heels? You might be one twenty without them, am I right? Or trifle with their clothes, hair styling, the gestures they use, the words they say, their country dialect etc.

BUT, it should be always funny, not offending. For instance, some time ago I had got acquainted with a model who had a blouse with artificial feathers. And I told her: "I hope they didn't harm some innocent birds to make your blouse..." She burst her sides with laughter.

Don't be arrogant, but amusing. Love yourself before the others, but don't be an egoist. Try to attend to your needs first, and then to the others' needs.

After you have talked with a girl (don't forget, looks, body language – posture, shoulders, gestures, and also your voice should be deep-toned and manly), tell her: "Do you know, I had a good time talking with you, but since I have no more time to talk, let us hear again. Do you have a phone at which I can find you? After you have taken her phone number just get away, there's no sense hanging like an idiot.

Several rules: don't give a damn what she is thinking at the moment. If you want to know what she thinks, you will be thinking for two and won't be able to concentrate. Have your rules. Don't tolerate infantile behaviour. Don't tolerate controlling behaviour by a woman. Don't tolerate rude behaviour or any other behaviour you don't like. If they behave like that, tell them you don't like it. If they complain, tell them to get away. This is a man.
You'll find out that most women will be silent as fish after you tell them something like that and will fawn on you like kittens.

When you call them for a date. First – no dinner, no flowers, no romantic. As I already mentioned, the manly and confident man chooses the place of the date while the dominating man not only chooses the place of the date, but chooses a plain one.

Invite her to a coffee or tea, or to go out shopping - something different and cheap. You don't want to go out with somebody, pay her the dinner and drinks and be left with

116

nothing afterwards, do you?

The way you ask about the date - I will be in the so and so café at such and such time, please, feel invited... You tell the place, time etc. You can first ask her what her schedule is and then choose the place and time.

Never leave her to choose. You must be a man and you must lead. Lead all the time – from the first date, through the phone all, to the second date, to bed. Lead all the time. After that, ask her whether she would appear at all because you don't like women who don't appear at dates.

Tell it to her simply and clearly. She must understand that she cannot waste your time – a real man's time.

When you meet, be cute, trifle with her etc. Make her come and take you from your place (instead of doing the opposite, taking her from her place) and go somewhere near to you (so as to be able to quickly take her to you afterwards).

Don't answer her questions directly, be always unclear. If she asks you how many women have you slept with, tell her: "You and my mother, but I'm not sure whether she counts." Funny, and besides, you don't give her direct answer. Or be frank, so that she doesn't know whether you are serious or not. For instance: "Well, I haven't dated women during the last three years, but this is because I have a crash on men."

"Where are you from?" Answer: "From Boston, but, are you asking me any dull questions?" "What do you do?" – "I'm a model and I do striptease at private parties..."

Reverse roles – pretend being tired of women taking you for a sexual object, not seeing the human creature inside you (this is something a woman would normally say, therefore it is super funny).

Touch her, laugh, behave as a cute and a nut. Don't share your feelings, don't tell how much you like her, because she will lose interest immediately.

Remember, women want challenge. Especially, if they are beautiful, they are used to men who fall in love with them pretty soon. Be different.

Then tell her "Come with me" and take her back home to you. Talk. There are two perfect ways to know when to kiss her. One is to start caressing her hair – if she accepts it gladly, it means you can do it for some more time and then kiss her. Or if she laughs at all funny things you are saying, leans much to you as if she likes you, then you may ask her "Do you want to kiss me?"

They would quite seldom say "Yes", sooner something like "Well, I don't know, I'm not sure. Then tell her "Well, let us try then" and kiss her. If she tells you firmly "NO", this means she won't kiss you. Then, don't try at all. Find another one.

So, you'll need a lot of training. Go out often, stop girls everywhere and talk to them. If you feel confused: first, this is normal. But you must do it despite fear. Start by talking to as many women as possible (old, young, ugly, beautiful, no matter) and simply have normal talk. Do it about 100-200 times and you will no longer feel fear or confusion. Then, you may start asking for the phone number and a date right there on the spot. If you think this is impossible, I will tell you I am a damn real example.

I felt it very difficult in the beginning, but I gave myself a vow that I will do anything possible to play better with women. Aim at the overall picture, not hitting on this girl exactly, but YOU feeling more comfortable with women in general.

And several last advice. Work continuously on yourself. Don't take refusals personally. Some women merely don't want to meet anyone right now. Be as it is. Take each refusal as a lesson teaching you how to manage better next time.

Never ask a woman's permission to do anything (kiss her or take her phone number, just be direct and brave). And admit that it will take you much time and work to become good. Months, years, admit it. There's no quick solution unless you look like Brad Pit.

And remember that women don't choose. You choose

them. Feel sexy and comfortable in your skin. Love yourself first, and then others. Don't find excuses for being a man and having a man's wants. Don't let anyone else make you feel bad for your convictions. Good luck.

After She's Already in Your Bed, Make Her Want You Again

Do you want to make maximum pleasure to your partner, no matter whether it is just a casual adventure or a lasting relation? It's not difficult.

You should just do what your instincts tell you, and what is most important – not be in a hurry...

Touch the woman you want, softly and tenderly in the beginning, like the touch of a breeze, on the lips, face, forehead, hair, ears, very softly...

Then, move slowly down the neck, very soft on the breasts and abdomen, let her feel your gasping breath on her skin, let her bristle up with the desire to get your lips touch...

And then, start kissing her – in the beginning, on some, say neutral places (though, at such a moment, no place is neutral) – again softly and tenderly, move slowly down to her breasts, abdomen and legs... Just soft kisses, like a hush before the storm – don't take off her clothes yet...

Then, try without undressing her to access some parts hidden under the clothes – for instance, if she wears a long-sleeved blouse – lift it gently upward to be able to touch and kiss the skin there... or even bite her slightly...

Now touch her more firmly, so that she feels your strength, but your softness too... Pass your hand over the places that attract you most – her round bottom, her rich breasts, squeeze slightly...

And follow continuously the effect of your actions – her breathing and her and the pupils of her eyes. If her pupils are already dilated and her breathing is slightly accelerated – grab her by the waist and press your lips against hers - eagerly, passionately, insatiably, stiffly, imperatively, but softly as well...

If she's not yet ready for it – then, go on kissing her on the lips, but softly, tenderly, as a game, play our tongue with hers, show her teasingly what you would like to do... Explore her hottest spots - not those that seem hot to you, but those, at the touch of which she reacts strongest...

This may be the usual places – ears, breasts, bottom. But they may either be not – it may be the base of the neck, the back – feel like an explorer of an unknown land and find them... The places that will make her moan with pleasure and be eager willing you to take her at last... which will make her extremely sensitive even for the slightest touch...

And don't be in a hurry – let her sink in the flames of passion, show her with your body the rhythm with which you want to love her, and then slowly, piece by piece, kissing each spot laid bare, strip her of her clothes... and yours, too...

Press slightly your hot body against her burning skin, but still don't be in a hurry to penetrate her... Now, unleash the element of your passion, kiss her quickly, fierily, persistently... Move your hands all around her body, feel with your fingers all secret places of her skin, all her cherished places...

Tease with your fingers or lips the nipples of her breasts, her clitoris... Thrust your fingers inside her and show her what you want to do with other parts of your body... (Naturally, you should do this only if your partner is ready – wet and excited.)

If you have still any clothes on, now take off everything and remain naked... In perfume only...

If you have something appropriate to use, you may try to spread her with it – ice-cream, natural juice, cream, chocolate... then, lick and suck what you have spread her with...

While still spread on, rub your body against hers, so that the ice-cream or cream sticks to you, too. Now, leave her to do the same for you – to explore your skin with her tongue, on your chest, abdomen, penis... Let her suck it in slightly, let her try to take it in her mouth as far as she can (but don't insist on her doing more than pleases her).

All the time she is kissing you touch her and kiss passionately all places accessible to you...

And then...

If your partner is active – put her onto yourself, but don't press things, leave her to fix, so that you can penetrate her. While she is moving, help her into coming in rhythm and stimulate her all the time – caress and squeeze (softly!) her breasts and bottom, and just as you want to hear the moans of her pleasure, she longs for yours, so, don't be ashamed and show her how excited she makes you...

If your partner prefers to be more passive (you could change this with greater encouragement), then, you can take the lead – place her the way you like, see once more whether she's ready and act...

Remember that most women need at least 15-20 minutes to cum vaginally (the best type of orgasm :)), and sometimes even more. Try to be up to it and carry on so long...

If you don't succeed the first time, try again. Even if you have the urge to finish, try to hold it as long as you can, so as to feel the pleasure of the real man – the one who can satisfy his woman... Believe me, your satisfaction will be at least as great as hers.

How Can You Hit On a Woman Depending on Her Zodiac Sign?

ARIES: As a beginning, don't forget that Aries is unusually punctual – never be late for a meeting. Agree with her about everything and don't lie to her. The sheep can be won easily by compliments and praises. She likes to be flattered and can be won easily by showing her how much you admire her. She is communicative and can be easily talked into. She likes polite men; for instance, she would like you to hold her coat and to open the door for her. A good-mannered man will impress her immediately. Don't forget to make her a lot of compliments, but not so much about her looks as about her skill, character and personal achievements. The Aries woman likes when her qualities are valued.

TAURUS: She is famous for her tenacity. With this sign, you can achieve your goal by mere hints only. Getting introduced to her, however, is a difficult task – she doesn't like new contacts. Don't try to take the lead of her anyway. If you want everything to be OK, you should give her proper care. The Taurus women are very hot and passionate; therefore, they prefer intelligent and yielding partners.

GEMINI: If you want to attract the Gemini's attention, show your interest for her, but don't be in a hurry. She prefers slight mystery and is taken up by topics unknown to her. Despite she sometimes looks frivolous and inconstant, she is quite prudent. She often misleads her partner showing enhanced interest for his person. With Gemini, this interest may only be an expression of their typical curiosity and not of some long-term plans in store. Give her the chance to talk and take up the role of the careful listener. In the end, she will be head and heels in love with you.

CANCER: A good start to be introduced to a Cancer is to ask her some advice. Never mention your previous girlfriends on a date. Wrap her with attention, but give her the chance to show her concern – this is what she needs. She is apt in wrapping men with her delicate clips, and she punished bad behaviour by squeezing some delicate place.

LION: She is definitely not an easy prey. Tell her that you need her. Always talk about her successes and achievements. You have a chance only if you talk about her superiority in everything. The woman never believes herself guilty and is never willing to change. Her partner must be the main subject of her pride. She's very jealous, but if you are faithful to her, she will reward you with much care and understanding. You may hit her on with sincere compliments.

VIRGO: Think out an ingenious and interesting topic for conversation. Be careful with the invitations to bars or restaurants because the Virgo woman doesn't like spending. Tell the Virgo your cherished wishes not with amorous look and delicate hints, but in plain text. Her sweetheart should have manly figure, prestigious car and brilliant social reputation. Virgo is the best master of various sexual techniques. You'll never be bored with her in bed and you can learn a lot from her.

LIBRA: When introduced to Libra, be ready to make compliments. Don't let any vulgarities at the meeting. Don't forget that all women born under this sign love luxury and comfort. Businessmen and military men have greatest chances. With Libra, you must live beautifully, comfortably, sometimes give flowers and serve coffee in bed. When you are with her, it is important to know that sex and flirt are quite different things.

SCORPIO: She' is unpredictable. To get introduced to her

you should be serious. Anyhow, if she laughs, you could laugh as well. Always ask her advice and be incredibly seducing. The Scorpio woman should get dressed long and much, and in the worst case - expensive. Scorpio is very passionate in erotic plays. The Scorpio sign features such qualities as greediness and the desire to make everything as it should.

SAGITTARIUS: Sagittarius woman remain free by soul. In order to be with a Sagittarius, offer her a walk in the park or a picnic. Never constrain her! Here, it is not enough to be a man in the physiological aspect. You should first become a Friend and an Adherent. There is one more condition – to be independent and to differ from the common mass by your unique individual abilities.

CAPRICORN: If you want acquaintance, you'd need wit. Give her an art piece as a present. Look super intelligent – Capricorn likes it! You may talk her into books or policy. Listen carefully to her and accept her opinion. Capricorns often show unostentatious tendency for feminism and unconventional sex forms.

AQUARIUS: Getting introduced to her is not an easy task. She likes discussing the recent events and various ideas. Don't forget to support her interests. Aquarius women like fashion very much and always look well. She will be very glad, if you pay her a compliment for her nice hair styling or elegant shoes.

PISCES: They are very touchy. Leave the conversation take the course Pisces want. They love parties, discos and compliments! They tend to lend the initiative in life and sex to their partner.

Why Women Fall in Love with Bad Boys?

Why women prefer bad boys? Have you asked yourself why beautiful women always fall in love just with this type of men? They say that they dream of Prince Charming on a white horse, but they fall in love with the bad boy. What is the reason? If we consider it, things are not so unclear.

The good boy knows how to dress and maintain himself. He is always tidy and clean. But it seems as if he is hiding something behind this perfect appearance. Maybe, this is confidence, which he compensated by his perfect outer appearance. While with bad boys, it's quite another thing. They are confident in all types of clothes – elegant or sports. They feel handsome and they really look handsome whatever they put on. They have proven to themselves that they are cute and they are not interested in other people's opinion. Women first like this type of boys and then complain of them. While the good boy may never hurt a woman, be handsome and not silly, but whenever he shows some woman that he likes her, she runs away from him as soon as possible. A friend of mine had perfect attitude for women and they'd always cut him off. Then he decided to change the tactic and started behaving rude to them. The result is that they still call on him even a year after they have broken off.

As I already mentioned, good boys are always afraid to take decisions and always leave it to the woman to decide where to go etc. This does not mean that they value a woman's opinion, but they simply find it easier. Transferring the responsibility to the woman the good boy washes his hands and is sure that, by doing so he will avoid unnecessary troubles. Bad boys know what they want and how to win it. They will take the woman to a place which will impress her greatly.

Good boys love to live easily and not burden themselves with someone else's problems. If the woman has any troubles, the good boy will find a reason to leave, not offering his help. Good boys just don't burden themselves with other people's problems. But whether a bad boy will help? It's not sure, but he sooner will do it for his own ego. He would like to feel as a real hero. And naturally, the woman will be grateful and pleased with your help. Thus, the bad boy wins a positive score.

Moreover, the good boy, however he may like a woman, will always be influenced by the opinion of his friends and relatives and the woman will often remain ignored and disappointed. She will never be able to count on him. With the bad boy, it is the same, but he will love the woman and will not give a damn about the others' opinion. He likes challenges and the hard way. He is independent and how much he loves his mother, he will prefer his friend to her.

The bad boy was bad yet in his childhood. He trained football, box, wrestling or something like that, while the good boy played the piano or participated in the dance ensemble. He doesn't love rows and he always tries to stay away from them. He doesn't like to argue with anybody and he thinks only about his personal calm. The bad boy has got accustomed to tell everything in plain text and has no problems with argues. He is prepared for anything in order to be respected. Such a man can always defend a woman. If somebody offends her, he is ready to jump at his feet and fight. While the good boy would prefer to settle the matter by talking and will not show strength in any way.

The bad boy is living now and for the moment. He doesn't think about the future, but would amuse himself right now. He likes crazy emotions. He is impulsive and he lives for the moment. He attracts life. And the woman likes to live and feel pleasure and experience emotions which a good boy cannot afford her. He lives for tomorrow and constantly makes plans. He always wants to change the woman, while the bad boy likes her the way she is.

The bad boy is unpredictable. He can surprise the woman in any way. He can, while they are going home along the street, grasp her by surprise, press her in some dark corner and start kissing her passionately, while you can't expect such things from the good boy. He is polite, he obeys order, and he is boring. He can't think of or sooner he won't do anything mad or interesting to move the woman.

Good boys envy bad ones in secret. They know that they can't perform like them and therefore, they often despise them. They know that they cannot be so confident as them, that they cannot manage with everything alone and that they cannot protect themselves. While bad boys don't give a damn what good boys think of them and don't count them as their rivals because they are sure that women will like them more.

Women feel within 10 seconds what kind of man is there in front of them, whether he is good or bad. If you ask them, they will tell you that the ideal man for them is a gentleman, gallant, with sense of humour etc. But the truth is quite different. They will have a crash on the self-confident type who won't show particular interest for them and will be dominating. Yet from school years, those who didn't give a damn about anything, didn't make the effort to learn anything, but were hanging about cafes, ultimately dated the most beautiful women.

Printed in the United Kingdom
by Lightning Source UK Ltd.
134736UK00001B/389/A